OAK PARK PUBLIC LIBRARY

31132 012 494 690

JAN - - 2013

OAK PARK PUBLIC LIBRARY

W9-DBG-830

MATH SMARTS!

Percent and Ratio SMARTS!

Lucille Caron
Philip M. St. Jacques

Enslow Publishers, Inc.
40 Industrial Road
Box 398
Berkeley Heights, NJ 07922
USA

http://www.enslow.com

Copyright © 2012 by Lucille Caron and Philip M. St. Jacques

All rights reserved.

No part of this book may be reproduced by any means without the written permission of the publisher.

Original edition published as *Percents and Ratios* in 2000.

Library of Congress Cataloging-in-Publication Data

Caron, Lucille.
  Percent and ratio smarts! / Lucille Caron and Philip M. St. Jacques.
    p. cm. — (Math smarts!)
  Summary: "Re-inforce classroom learning of important percent and ratio skills including reducing ratios, the golden rectangle, and the meaning of percents"—Provided by publisher.
  Includes index.
  ISBN 978-0-7660-3940-7
  1. Fractions—Juvenile literature. 2. Ratio and proportion—Juvenile literature. I. St. Jacques, Philip M. II. Title.
  QA117.C379 2012
  513.2'6—dc22

2011008164

Paperback ISBN: 978-1-59845-317-1

Printed in China

052011 Leo Paper Group, Heshan City, Guangdong, China.

10 9 8 7 6 5 4 3 2 1

To Our Readers: We have done our best to make sure all Internet addresses in this book were active and appropriate when we went to press. However, the author and the publisher have no control over and assume no liability for the material available on those Internet sites or on other Web sites they may link to. Any comments or suggestions can be sent by e-mail to comments@enslow.com or to the address on the back cover.

Cover Illustration: © Shutterstock.com

Contents

Introduction

If you were to look up the meaning of the word *mathematics,* you would find that it is the study of numbers, quantities, and shapes, and how they relate to each other.

Mathematics is important to all world cultures, including our world of work. The following are just some of the ways in which studying math will help you:

► You will know how much money you are spending at the store.

► You will know if the cashier has given you the right change.

► You will know how to use measurements to build things.

► Your science classes will be easier and more interesting.

► You will understand music on a whole new level.

► You will be empowered to qualify for and land a rewarding job.

Percents and ratios are an important part of life. Test grades and stock market changes are written as percents. You need to know percents when you calculate a tip for your waiter or waitress. Knowing ratios makes it possible to change a recipe that calls for one part oatmeal to half part water.

This book has been written so that you can learn about percents and ratios at your own speed. Use it on your own, or with the help of a friend, tutor, or parent.

Good luck and have fun!

The Meaning of Ratios

A ratio is the comparison between two quantities or numbers. Ratios are used to compare ages, prices, distances, or time. They are important for making and reading maps, blueprints, and other models; for finding the best bargain; and for judging the fastest competitor.

Writing Ratios

Ratios can be written in three different ways:

1. A colon may be used to write a ratio. (:)
2. A fraction bar may be used to write a ratio. (—)
3. The word *to* may be used to write a ratio. (to)

Suppose there are 10 boys and 12 girls in a class. You can write the ratio of the number of boys to the number of girls in three different ways:

1. With a colon: 10:12
2. As a fraction: $\frac{10}{12}$
3. In words: 10 to 12

Although a ratio can be written in three different ways, it is always read the same way.

You read each of the three above ratios as "ten to twelve."

A **ratio** is used to compare two or more quantities.

Terms

The numbers in a ratio are called terms. In the previous ratio, 10 to 12, ten is the first term and twelve is the second term.

Identify the terms in 8 to 12		Identify the terms in 4:3	
First term:	8	First term:	4
Second term:	12	Second term:	3

Order

The order of the terms is important when writing ratios.

A pet store has 12 dogs and 6 puppies. You can write either the ratio of dogs to puppies or the ratio of puppies to dogs.

To find the ratio of dogs to puppies, write the term for dogs (12) and place it over the term for puppies (6).

$$\frac{12}{6} \quad \textbf{dogs} \\ \textbf{puppies}$$

This can also be written as: 12:6   or   12 to 6

On the other hand, the ratio of puppies to dogs is

$$\frac{6}{12} \quad \textbf{puppies} \\ \textbf{dogs}$$ or 6:12   or   6 to 12

Is $\frac{12}{6}$ the same as $\frac{6}{12}$? Compare the terms in the two ratios.

Identify the terms in the ratio $\frac{12}{6}$:

first term: 12
second term: 6

Identify the terms in the ratio $\frac{6}{12}$:

first term: 6
second term: 12

The terms are not the same in the above ratios.

terms — The numbers in a ratio.

2 Reducing Ratios

Ratios can be used to compare the lifespans of different animals. For example, a zoologist might compare the average lifespan of a giant panda to that of a wolf, an Asiatic lion, or a giant tortoise. The giant panda lives for an average of 15 years, the wolf has a lifespan of 10 years, the Asiatic lion lives to 30 years, and the giant tortoise has a lifespan of 190 years.

Ratios can show how many times greater or smaller one number is than another.

How many times greater is the lifespan of an Asiatic lion than a giant panda? Before solving this problem, look at the procedure for reducing ratios.

Reducing Ratios to Lowest Terms

Reduce 9:18 to lowest terms.

Step 1: Divide both terms by the largest number that will evenly divide both terms.

$9 \div 9 : 18 \div 9$

Step 2: Reduce to lowest terms.

$1 : 2$

9 to 18 reduces to 1 to 2.

A ratio is in lowest terms when both terms are whole numbers and no other whole number except for 1 can evenly divide both terms.

Reducing ratios is just like reducing fractions!
Reducing 9:18 is the same as reducing $\frac{9}{18}$.

Write the ratio of the lifespan of an Asiatic lion to that of a giant panda in lowest terms.

Step 1: Write the ratio.   30 to 15

Step 2: Divide the first and second   30 ÷ 15 to 15 ÷ 15
term by the largest number
that will evenly divide both terms.

Step 3: Reduce to lowest terms.   2 to 1

The ratio 2 to 1 means that the Asiatic lion has a lifespan that is 2 times longer than that of the giant panda.

How many times longer is the lifespan of a giant tortoise than that of a wolf?

Step 1: Write the ratio.   190 to 10

Step 2: Divide the first and second   190 ÷ 10 to 10 ÷ 10
terms by the largest number
that will evenly divide both
of them.

Step 3: Reduce to lowest terms.   19 to 1

The ratio 19 to 1 means that the giant tortoise has a lifespan that is 19 times longer than that of the wolf.

When both terms in a ratio cannot be divided by a whole number other than 1, the ratio is in its **lowest terms**.

A percent is a ratio that compares a number to one hundred. Remember, a ratio has two terms. When a percent is written as a ratio, the second term is always 100.

For example: 50% means 50 out of 100.
    The first term is 50. The second term is 100.
    The percent symbol (%) means "per one hundred."

A percent can be written as a ratio in three different ways:

1. Using a colon: 50:100

2. Using a fraction bar: $\frac{50}{100}$

3. Using the word *to*:   50 to 100

Write 50 to 100 in lowest terms.

Step 1: Write the ratio.   50 to 100

Step 2: Divide the first and second   50 ÷ 50 to 100 ÷ 50
             terms by the largest number
             that will evenly divide both
             of them.

Step 3: Reduce to lowest terms.   1 to 2

This isn't so hard.

A **percent** is a ratio whose second term is 100.

First Term

A percent compares a number to 100. The number is always the first term. The first term can be less than 100, equal to 100, or greater than 100. The second term is always 100.

Example of a First Term Less than 100

Write 35% as a ratio.

In words: 35 to 100

Thirty-five is the first term and it is less than 100.

Thirty-five percent is read as "35 out of 100."

Reduce to lowest terms: 35 ÷ 5 to 100 ÷ 5

7 to 20

Example of a First Term Equal to 100

Write 100% as a ratio.

In words: 100 to 100

One hundred is the first term and it is equal to 100.

The first term is equal to the second term.

Reduce to lowest terms: 100 ÷ 100 to 100 ÷ 100

The ratio is equal to one.   1 to 1

Example of a First Term Greater than 100

Write 300% as a ratio.

In words: 300 to 100

Three hundred is the first term and it is greater than 100.

Reduce to lowest terms   300 ÷ 100 to 100 ÷ 100

3 to 1

The first term is 3 times greater than the second term.

The percent symbol, %, is 100 written in a special way.

$$\frac{50}{100} = 50:100 = 50\%$$

Equivalent ratios are ratios that are equal in value. They are useful for determining missing quantities.

Suppose your neighborhood has 64 streetlights on every 8 blocks. How many streetlights are there on 1 block? on 16 blocks? Use equivalent ratios to find the answers to these problems.

Renaming a Ratio in Lowest Terms

Remember, to rename a ratio in lowest terms, divide the first and second terms by the largest number that will evenly divide both terms.

How many streetlights are there on one block?

The question tells you that the second term of the equivalent ratio needs to be 1 (for *one* block).

Step 1: Write the known ratio of streetlights to blocks.

64 to 8
streetlights to blocks

Step 2: Divide the first and second terms by the second term, so that the second term of the equivalent ratio will be 1.

64 ÷ 8 to 8 ÷ 8

Step 3: Write the equivalent ratio. There are 8 streetlights on 1 block.

8 to 1

8 to 1 and **64 to 8** have the same value. They are equivalent ratios.

Ratios are equivalent when their fractions are equal. The ratio 30:40 and the ratio 3:4 are equivalent because their fractions $\frac{30}{40}$ and $\frac{3}{4}$ are equal.

Renaming a Ratio in Higher Terms

To rename a ratio in higher terms, multiply both terms by the same number.

How many streetlights are there on 16 blocks?

The question tells you that the second term of the equivalent ratio needs to be 16.

Step 1: Write the known ratio of streetlights to blocks.

64 to 8

Step 2: Look at the second term (8). What number multiplied by 8 will give 16 in the second term of the equivalent ratio? (2)

multiples of 8: 8, 16, . . .

Step 3: Multiply each term by 2.

64×2 to 8×2

128 to 16

There are 128 streetlights on 16 blocks.

The reduced ratio of 8 to 1 would also give the same answer.

The second term is one. You are looking for the number of streetlights on 16 blocks. Sixteen times one equals 16 blocks.

Step 1: Write the reduced ratio.

8 to 1

Step 2: Multiply each term by 16.

8×16 to 1×16

128 to 16

Notice that the answers are the same. 8 to 1, 64 to 8, and 128 to 16 are all equivalent ratios.

Multiplying or dividing both terms of a ratio by the same number will not change the value of the ratio.

Sometimes, the numbers in a ratio have the same units. For example, the terms in the ratio of length to width, such as 20 feet to 80 feet, have the same units. A rate is a ratio that compares numbers with two different units. For example, the rate of the price of gold is about $\frac{285 \text{ dollars}}{1 \text{ ounce}}$. Other rates are miles per hour and feet per second.

Rates can compare several different qualities, a few of which are listed here.

1. **Length**, which can be expressed in feet, meters, miles . . .
2. **Mass**, which can be expressed in grams, ounces, pounds . . .
3. **Time**, which can be expressed in days, hours, minutes . . .
4. **Monetary value**, which can be expressed in dollars, cents, francs . . .

Terms

Rates can be written in two different ways:

1. Using a fraction bar: (−) $\dfrac{\$285}{1 \text{ ounce}}$

2. Using words: *per*   285 dollars per 1 ounce

A fraction bar or the word *per* compares the two units. For example, bananas are sold at the rate of 79 cents per 2 pounds.

Using words: 79 cents per 2 pounds

Using a fraction bar: $\dfrac{79 \text{ cents}}{2 \text{ pounds}}$

A **rate** is a special kind of ratio. The only difference is in the type of units of each term. In a rate, the units of the two terms are different.

Reducing Rates to Lowest Terms

If a dozen donuts sells for $4.80, how much does one donut cost?

To find the cost of one donut, divide the numerator and the denominator by the denominator. The answer is an equivalent ratio with the second term of 1.

Step 1: Write the rate.

$$\frac{\$4.80}{12 \text{ donuts}}$$

Step 2: Divide the numerator and denominator by the denominator.

$$\frac{\$4.80 \div 12}{12 \text{ donuts} \div 12}$$

$$12\overline{)4.80} \quad 12\overline{)12}$$

0.40
12)4.80
− 4 8
0

1
12)12
− 12
0

Step 3: Write the rate. The rate is now in lowest terms.

$0.40 per 1 donut

Each donut costs 40 cents.

Go to your local bagel shop or look in newspaper ads to find out the price of a dozen bagels. Find the cost of one bagel by reducing the rate to lowest terms.

Bagels for Sale

Remember: A ratio is in lowest terms when both terms are whole numbers and no other number except for 1 can evenly divide both terms (see page 8).

Your best friend has 3 quarters, and you have 2 dimes and 1 nickel. He tells you he has twice as much money as you have. Is he correct? Use ratios to compare your friend's amount to your amount.

Money

To find the ratio of different units of measure, first express both numbers in the same units of measure.

Step 1: Write a ratio comparing your best friend's money to your money. $\dfrac{3 \text{ quarters}}{2 \text{ dimes, 1 nickel}}$

Step 2: Express both terms in the same units. (Change both terms to cents.)

$$3 \text{ quarters} = 75 \text{ cents}$$
$$2 \text{ dimes, 1 nickel} = 25 \text{ cents}$$

Step 3: Write the ratio using the same units.

$$\frac{75 \text{ cents}}{25 \text{ cents}}$$

Step 4: Reduce the ratio to lowest terms. The units cancel out.

$$\frac{75 \text{ cents}}{25 \text{ cents}} = \frac{3 \text{ cents}}{1 \text{ cents}}$$

$$25\overline{)75} \quad \begin{array}{r} 3 \\ -75 \\ \hline 0 \end{array} \quad 3 \text{ to } 1$$

Your friend was incorrect. The ratio shows that your friend has three times as much money as you do, not twice as much.

When a fraction contains the same units, such as cents, in the numerator and the denominator, you can drop them. They cancel each other out.

Time

You can do your homework in 2 hours. Your sister does her homework in 20 minutes. What is the ratio of your homework time to your sister's homework time?

Step 1: Write a ratio comparing your homework time to your sister's time.

$$2 \text{ hours to } 20 \text{ minutes}$$

Step 2: Express both terms in the same units. (Change hours to minutes.)

$$2 \text{ hours} = 2 \times 60 \text{ minutes} = 120 \text{ minutes}$$

Step 3: Write the ratio using the same units.

$$120 \text{ minutes to } 20 \text{ minutes}$$

Step 4: Reduce the ratio to lowest terms. The units cancel out.

$$\frac{120 \text{ minutes}}{20 \text{ minutes}} = \frac{6 \text{ minutes}}{1 \text{ minutes}}$$

$$\begin{array}{r} 6 \\ 20\overline{)120} \\ -120 \\ \hline 0 \end{array}$$

6 to 1

The ratio means that you spend 6 times as much time doing your homework as your sister does.

When ratios are used for comparison, like comparing homework time with homework time, the units must be the same.

A cookie recipe calls for $\frac{1}{2}$ cup of sugar and $\frac{2}{3}$ cup of walnuts. What is the ratio of the amount of sugar to the amount of walnuts? (This will be useful if you want to double the recipe but don't know if you have enough ingredients.)

Expressing Fractions as Whole Number Ratios

A fraction can be expressed as a ratio by changing both terms to whole numbers.

Step 1: Write the ratio of cups of sugar to cups of walnuts.

$$\frac{1}{2} \text{ to } \frac{2}{3}$$

Step 2: Find the least common multiple (LCM) of the denominators.

multiples of 2: 2, 4, **6**, 8, . . .

multiples of 3: 3, **6**, 9, 12, . . .   LCM = 6

Step 3: Multiply each term by the LCM.

$$\frac{1}{2} \times 6 \text{ to } \frac{2}{3} \times 6$$

$$\frac{6}{2} \text{ to } \frac{12}{3}$$

Step 4: Reduce the ratio to   3 to 4
lowest terms.

The ratio of the amount of sugar to the amount of walnuts is 3 to 4.

least common multiple (LCM) — The smallest number that appears in both sets of multiples for two numbers.

Expressing Mixed Numbers as Whole Number Ratios

The same recipe calls for $1\frac{1}{8}$ cups of milk and $2\frac{3}{4}$ cups of flour. What is the ratio of the amount of milk to the amount of flour?

Step 1: Write the ratio of cups of milk to cups of flour.

$$1\frac{1}{8} \text{ to } 2\frac{3}{4}$$

Step 2: Change the mixed numbers to improper fractions.

$$\frac{(1 \times 8) + 1}{8} \text{ to } \frac{(2 \times 4) + 3}{4}$$

$$\frac{9}{8} \text{ to } \frac{11}{4}$$

Step 3: Find the LCM of the denominators.

multiples of 8: **8**, 16, 24, . . .

multiples of 4: 4, **8**, 12, . . .   LCM = 8

Step 4: Multiply each term by the LCM.

$$\frac{9}{8} \times 8 \text{ to } \frac{11}{4} \times 8$$

Step 5: Reduce the ratio to lowest terms.

$$\frac{9}{\underset{1}{\cancel{8}}} \times \overset{1}{\cancel{8}} \text{ to } \frac{11}{\underset{1}{\cancel{4}}} \times \overset{2}{\cancel{8}}$$

$$\frac{9}{1} \text{ to } \frac{11 \times 2}{1}$$

9 to 22

The ratio of the amount of milk to the amount of flour is 9 to 22. Every time you use 9 parts milk, you use 22 parts flour.

Whole numbers are all the counting numbers and zero:
0, 1, 2, 3, 4, 5, 6, . . .

Suppose you jumped 5.2 feet and your friend jumped 2.6 feet. How many times farther did you jump?

Step 1: Write the ratio of your jump length to your friend's jump length.

$$\frac{5.2 \text{ ft.}}{2.6 \text{ ft.}}$$

Step 2: Count the number of decimal places in each term.

5.2	one decimal place
2.6	one decimal place

Step 3: Find the greatest power of ten using the table on the next page.

number	decimal places	multiply by
5.2	1	10
2.6	1	10

Step 4: Multiply each term by 10. $\frac{5.2 \times 10}{2.6 \times 10} = \frac{52}{26}$

Step 5: Reduce the ratio to lowest terms. Drop the units.

$$\frac{52 \text{ ft.}}{26 \text{ ft.}} = \frac{2}{1}, \text{ or 2 to 1}$$

2 to 1

The ratio 2 to 1 means that 5.2 is twice as large as 2.6 and that you can jump twice as far as your friend.

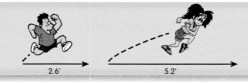

2.6'   5.2'

Decimal Places in the Number	Multiply by
0	1
1	10
2	100
3	1,000
4	10,000
5	100,000
6	1,000,000

Write 0.0028 to 0.00014 as a ratio of whole numbers.

Step 1: Count the number of decimal places in each term.

0.0028	4 decimal places
0.00014	5 decimal places

Step 2: The greatest number of decimal places is 5. Look at the table. Multiply each term by 100,000.

$$0.0028 \times 100,000 \text{ to } 0.00014 \times 100,000$$

$$280 \text{ to } 14$$

Step 3: Reduce the ratio to lowest terms.

$$\frac{280}{14} = \frac{20}{1}, \text{ or } 20 \text{ to } 1$$

Run the 100-yard dash with a friend. Write the ratio of your time to your friend's time. Reduce the ratio to lowest terms.

An easy way to remember the table above: If there are 5 decimal places, multiply by 100,000, because there are five zeros in 100,000.

9 Unit Pricing

Shoppers use unit pricing to make comparisons between prices. Items are packaged in different sizes, and shoppers must decide which size gives them the best bargain. Unit pricing is a rate that compares an item's cost to its quantity.

Finding the Better Buy

What is the better buy, 4 Ping-Pong balls for $4.98 or 7 for $8.50?

Step 1: Write the rate of cost per quantity as a fraction.

$$\frac{\$4.98}{4 \text{ balls}} \qquad \frac{\$8.50}{7 \text{ balls}}$$

Step 2: Divide to the nearest thousandths.

```
      1.245              1.214
   4)4.980            7)8.500
    − 4                − 7
    ───                ───
      9                  15
    − 8                − 14
    ───                ───
     18                  10
   − 16                 − 7
    ───                ───
     20                  30
   − 20                − 28
    ───                ───
      0                   2
```

Step 3: Round to the nearest cent.

$1.245   rounds to $1.25

$1.214   rounds to $1.21

The better buy is 7 Ping-Pong balls for $8.50. At that rate, one ball costs $1.21.

Unit price is the price for a particular size of food, such as $2.00 per pound of tomatoes. The cost per unit is a great way to compare prices of different brands of food.

What is the better buy: a 16-ounce box of cereal that costs $3.86 or a 20-ounce box of cereal that costs $4.90?

Step 1: Write the rate of cost to quantity as a fraction.

$$\frac{\$3.86}{16 \text{ oz.}} \qquad \frac{\$4.90}{20 \text{ oz.}}$$

Step 2: Divide to the nearest thousandths.

```
    0.241              0.245
16)3.860           20)4.900
  - 3 2              - 4 0
    66                 90
  - 64              - 80
    20                100
  - 16             - 100
     4                  0
```

Step 3: Round to the nearest cent.

$0.241   rounds to $0.24 per oz.
$0.245   rounds to $0.25 per oz.

The better buy is the 16-ounce box of cereal. One ounce of cereal in that box costs only 24 cents.

Go to your local supermarket and find the unit price of your favorite cereal. What is the unit price for the same cereal in a smaller or larger quantity? What is the better buy?

Rounding a number is a way of writing the number with fewer digits.

A proportion is an equation that shows two ratios. A true proportion is an equation that shows two equivalent ratios. A proportion can be written in two different ways.

1. Using fractions: $\frac{4}{2} = \frac{16}{8}$

2. Using colons: $4:2 = 16:8$

The proportion is read, "4 is to 2 as 16 is to 8." A proportion has four terms. The four terms of the above proportion are 4, 2, 16, and 8. Every proportion can be written as a multiplication equation.

Proportion: $\frac{4}{2} \diagdown\diagup \frac{16}{8}$

Multiplication equation: $4 \times 8 = 2 \times 16$
$$32 = 32$$

The two products, of 4×8 and of 2×16, are called cross products. The cross products are found by multiplying the diagonals of the proportion. If the cross products are equal, the ratios are equal, and the proportion is called a true proportion. In the above example, the cross products are equal: $32 = 32$.

Are the following ratios equal? $\frac{2}{4}$ and $\frac{6}{8}$

Step 1: Write a proportion using the two ratios.

$\frac{2}{4} \overset{?}{=} \frac{6}{8}$

Step 2: Write the proportion as a multiplication equation.

$2 \times 8 \overset{?}{=} 4 \times 6$

A **proportion** is an equation that shows two ratios.

Step 3: Multiply. $16 \neq 24$

If the cross products are not equal, then the ratios are not equal.

Finding an Unknown Term

If you bike 8 miles in 2 hours, how far will you bike at the same rate in 3 hours?

Let's solve this problem using a proportion. There are three terms in this problem, 8 miles, 2 hours, and 3 hours. We have two terms with hours and just one term with miles. The missing term is in miles. When setting up a proportion, place the terms in the ratios in the same order.

Step 1: Write the first ratio. $\dfrac{8 \text{ miles}}{2 \text{ hours}}$

Step 2: Write the second ratio. $\dfrac{n \text{ miles}}{3 \text{ hours}}$
Let n represent the missing term.

Step 3: Write a proportion. $\dfrac{8 \text{ miles}}{2 \text{ hours}} = \dfrac{n \text{ miles}}{3 \text{ hours}}$

Step 4: Find the cross products. $8 \times 3 = 2 \times n$

$24 = 2n$

Step 5: Divide both sides by 2 $\dfrac{\overset{12}{\cancel{24}}}{\cancel{2}} = \dfrac{\cancel{2}n}{\cancel{2}}$
to solve for n.

$12 = n$

In 3 hours you will bike 12 miles.

Cross multiplication can tell you if the proportions are equal. If the cross products are equal, so is the proportion.

In a class, the ratio of the number of chairs to the number of desks is 8 to 3. If there are 15 desks in the class, how many chairs are there?

Find the number of chairs in the class.

Step 1: Write the known ratio.

$$\frac{\text{chairs}}{\text{desks}} = \frac{8}{3}$$

Step 2: Write the second ratio. Let x stand for the unknown number of chairs.

$$\frac{\text{chairs}}{\text{desks}} = \frac{x}{15}$$

Step 3: Set the two ratios equal to one another.

$$\frac{8}{3} = \frac{x}{15}$$

Step 4: Multiply to find cross products.

$$\frac{8}{3} \diagup\!\!\!\!\diagdown \frac{x}{15}$$

$$3x = 8 \times 15$$

$$3x = 120$$

Step 5: Divide both sides by 3 to solve for x.

$$\frac{\cancel{3}x}{\cancel{3}} = \frac{120}{3}$$

$$x = 40$$

There are 40 chairs in the class.

Usually, the missing term in a proportion is represented by a letter. You can check your result by replacing the letter with your answer: $\frac{8}{3} = \frac{40}{15}$ is a true proportion. It checks.

The ratio of a daughter's age to her mother's age is 2 to 5. If the daughter is 14 years old, how old is the mother?

Find the mother's age.

Step 1: Write the known ratio.

$$\frac{\text{daughter}}{\text{mother}} = \frac{2}{5}$$

Step 2: Write the second ratio. Let x equal the mother's age.

$$\frac{\text{daughter}}{\text{mother}} = \frac{14}{x}$$

Step 3: Set the two ratios equal to one another.

$$\frac{2}{5} = \frac{14}{x}$$

Step 4: Multiply to find cross products.

$$\frac{2}{5} \diagdown\!\!\!\diagup \frac{14}{x}$$

$$2x = 5 \times 14$$

$$2x = 70$$

Step 5: Divide both sides by 2 to solve for x.

$$\frac{2x}{2} = \frac{70}{2}$$

$$x = 35$$

The mother is 35 years old.

Find the ratio of your age to the age of someone else in your family. Reduce the ratio to lowest terms.

Check your answer: Replace x with your answer, 35.

$$\frac{2}{5} = \frac{14}{x} \quad \frac{2}{5} = \frac{14}{35}$$

It checks.

Architects, engineers, and illustrators use scale drawings when they plan buildings and drawings. A scale drawing represents either an increase or decrease in the size of the actual object.

Reduction

The tallest land animal is the giraffe. When illustrators have to draw such a large animal in a small space, such as a notebook page, they use a scale that will make the drawing similar to but smaller than the actual object.

Suppose the illustrator draws a picture of a giraffe that has a height of $2\frac{1}{4}$ inches. Under the picture of the giraffe the illustrator writes the following scale: $\frac{1}{8}$ inch $= 1$ foot.

What is the actual height of the giraffe?

Step 1: Write the ratio of picture height to actual height.

$$\frac{\frac{1}{8} \text{ inch}}{1 \text{ foot}}$$

Step 2: Write the second ratio. Let x equal the actual height of the giraffe.

$$\frac{2\frac{1}{4} \text{ inch}}{x}$$

Step 3: Change the mixed number in the second ratio to an improper fraction.

$$\frac{\frac{9}{4} \text{ inch}}{x}$$

Step 4: Set the two ratios equal to each other.

$$\frac{\frac{1}{8}}{1} = \frac{\frac{9}{4}}{x}$$

A **scale** is a ratio that compares the dimensions of a model to the dimensions of an object.

Step 5: Multiply to find cross products.

$$\frac{1}{8}x = \frac{9}{4}$$

Step 6: Multiply both sides by 8 to solve for x.

$$8 \times \frac{1}{8}x = \frac{9}{4} \times \overset{2}{8} \qquad 1x = 18 \qquad x = 18$$

The actual height of the giraffe is 18 feet.

Enlargement

Suppose the illustrator now draws a 3-inch-long picture of an ant. Under the picture of the ant, the illustrator writes the following scale: $\frac{1}{2}$ inch = 1 mm. A millimeter is much smaller than an inch.

What is the actual length of the ant?

You can use ratios to solve this problem.

Step 1: Write the known ratio.

$$\frac{1}{2} = 0.5$$

$$\frac{\text{inch}}{\text{mm}} = \frac{0.5}{1}$$

Step 2: Write the second ratio.
Let x equal the ant's length.

$$\frac{\text{inch}}{\text{mm}} = \frac{3}{x}$$

Step 3: Set the two ratios equal to one another.

$$\frac{0.5}{1} = \frac{3}{x}$$

Step 4: Multiply to find cross products.

$$\frac{0.5}{1} \diagup\!\!\!\!\diagdown \frac{3}{x}$$
$$0.5x = 3$$

Step 5: Divide by 0.5 to solve for x.

$$\frac{0.5x}{0.5} \diagup\!\!\!\!\diagdown \frac{3}{0.5}$$
$$x = 6$$

The actual length of the ant is 6 mm.

In an **enlargement** or **reduction,** a scale is used to produce a similar shape.

Ratios can be applied to architecture. The Parthenon is an example of Greek architecture. It was built in the 5th century B.C. on the Acropolis at Athens. The front of the building is a golden rectangle. The ratio of the length of the golden rectangle to its width is approximately 1.6 to 1. This means that the length is about 1.6 times the width.

Finding the Width of a Golden Rectangle

If a picture frame is 46.4 inches long, find the width if the frame is a golden rectangle.

To find the width of a golden rectangle, divide the length by 1.6.

Step 1: Divide the length by 1.6. $46.4 \div 1.6$

Step 2: Move the decimal place one place to the right in the divisor and in the dividend.

$$\begin{array}{r} 29 \\ 16\overline{)464} \\ -32 \\ \hline 144 \\ -144 \\ \hline 0 \end{array}$$

The width is 29 inches.

To check your answer write the ratio of length to width and reduce the ratio to lowest terms.

Step 1: Write the ratio of length to width.   46.4 to 29

Step 2: Divide both terms by 29. $46.4 \div 29$ to $29 \div 29$
                                                           1.6 to 1

The ratio of length to width is 1.6 to 1. The width is correct.

The **golden rectangle** is a very special rectangle. It is considered to have a very pleasing ratio of length to width. The ratio is about 1.6 to 1.

Finding the Length of a Golden Rectangle

A picture frame is 15 inches wide. Find the length if the frame is a golden rectangle.

Multiply the width by 1.6.

$$\begin{array}{r} 1\,5 \\ \times\ 1.6 \\ \hline 9\,0 \\ +\ 1\,5 \\ \hline 2\,4.0 \end{array}$$

The length is 24 inches.

To check your answer, write the ratio of length to width and divide.

Step 1: Write the ratio of length to width.　　24 to 15

Step 2: Divide both terms by the second term.

$$24 \div 15 \text{ to } 15 \div 15$$

$$\begin{array}{r} 1.6 \\ 15\overline{)24.0} \\ -\,15 \\ \hline 90 \\ -\,90 \\ \hline 0 \end{array} \qquad \begin{array}{r} 1 \\ 15\overline{)15} \end{array}$$

The ratio of length to width is 1.6 to 1. The length is correct.

Measure one of the picture frames in your house. Write the ratio of length to width. Reduce the ratio by dividing each term by the width. Is it a golden rectangle?

Artist Leonardo da Vinci used the ratio of the golden rectangle in his works.

Probability is the chance that an event will or will not occur, such as a 20 percent chance of rain. Probability can be expressed as a ratio. To find the probability of an event, write the number of ways that event can occur out of the total number of possible outcomes.

$$\text{Probability (Event)} = \frac{\text{number of ways an event can occur}}{\text{number of all possible outcomes}}$$

If you flip a penny, what is the probability of getting a tail?

Look at the following steps:

Step 1: List the possible outcomes.　　**tails and heads**

Step 2: Count the number of all possible outcomes.

total outcomes = tails + heads
total outcomes = 2

Step 3: How many ways can a tail occur when you flip a penny?
one way

Step 4: Write the ratio of the number of ways a tail can occur to the total number of outcomes.

Probability of tails $= \frac{1}{2}$

P (tails) $= \frac{1}{2}$ is read as "the probability of getting a tail is one in two."

The **probability** of an event is a number between 0 and 1. A probability of zero means it will not happen. A probability of 1 means it will definitely happen.

There are 6 numbers on the faces of a die: 1, 2, 3, 4, 5, and 6. Roll a die. What is the probability of rolling an odd number?

Step 1: List all the possible outcomes.

1, 2, 3, 4, 5, and 6

Step 2: Count the number of all the possible outcomes in Step 1.

total possible outcomes = 6

Step 3: List all the ways of rolling an odd number.

odd numbers = 1, 3, 5

Step 4: Count the number of ways of rolling an odd number.

number of odd numbers = 3

Step 5: Write the ratio of the number of ways of rolling an odd number to the total number of outcomes.

$$P \text{ (odd number)} = \frac{3}{6}$$

Step 6: Reduce the ratio to lowest terms.

$$P \text{ (odd number)} = \frac{3 \div 3}{6 \div 3} = \frac{1}{2}$$

The probability of rolling an odd number is $\frac{1}{2}$ (one in two).

Flip a penny 100 times. How many times did heads occur? tails? Find the probability of getting a tail (see page 32). Write the ratio of the number of times a tail occurred to the number of times you flipped the coin (100). Reduce the ratio to lowest terms. Is this ratio equal to $\frac{1}{2}$?

If $\frac{1}{3}$ of the possible outcomes makes a statement true, the statement will be true in about $\frac{1}{3}$ of a large number of selections.

Percents can represent test scores, survey results, or sales tax. The word *percent* comes from the Latin words *per centum*, which mean "per hundred." The symbol for percent is %.

A percent compares a number to 100. The number can be less than 100, equal to 100, or greater than 100.

The list below shows the results for 100 test questions. The letter C stands for "correct" and I for "incorrect."

C	C	C	C	C	C	I	C	C	C
C	C	C	C	C	I	C	C	C	C
C	I	C	C	C	C	C	C	C	C
C	C	C	C	I	C	C	C	C	C
C	C	I	C	C	C	C	C	C	C
C	C	C	I	C	C	C	C	C	C
C	C	C	C	C	C	C	I	C	C
C	C	C	C	C	C	C	C	I	C
C	C	C	C	C	C	C	C	C	C
C	C	C	C	C	C	C	C	C	I

What percent of the 100 questions were answered incorrectly?
Count all the Is. There are nine Is. Nine out of 100 questions were answered incorrectly, or 9% of the answers were incorrect.

What percent of the 100 questions were answered correctly?
Count all the Cs. Since there are ninety-one Cs, 91 out of the 100 questions were answered correctly, or 91% were correct.

If you get a score of 100%, it means that you answered all the questions correctly.

Think of a percent as a ratio whose second term is 100.
For example, $40\% = 40{:}100$ or $\frac{40}{100}$

Models of Percents

You can use a model to show percents. What does 50% represent?

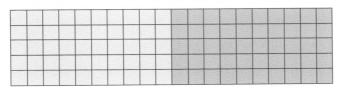

In the model, 50 of the squares are shaded in. This represents 50%.

What does 100% represent? Use the same model and shade in 100 squares. This model represents 1 whole.

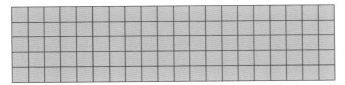

What does 150% represent? Use two models. In the first model, shade in 100 squares. In the second model, shade in 50 squares. This represents more than 1 whole.

Model 1

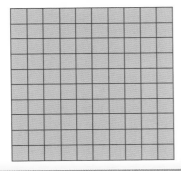

Model 2

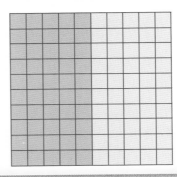

Percentages greater than 100 are like improper fractions.

$$150\% \text{ is } \frac{150}{100}, \text{ or } \frac{15}{10}, \text{ or } \frac{3}{2}$$

You can change a ratio to a percent or a percent to a ratio.

Changing a Ratio to a Percent When the Second Term Is 100

Suppose 75 of the 100 books in your library are science books. What percent of the books are science books?

Draw a model. Make 100 squares and shade in 75.

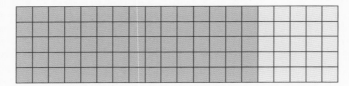

Step 1: Write the ratio in words.   75 out of 100

Step 2: To change the ratio to a   75 is the first term
percent, write the first
term and replace the   100 is the second term
second term (100) with
a percent symbol.   75%

75% of the books in the library are science books.

How many books in the library are not science books?

How many squares are not shaded in the model?

Twenty-five out of the 100 squares are not shaded. Therefore, 25% of the books are not science books.

When the second term of a ratio is 100, you can drop it and replace it with the percent symbol.

$$\frac{15}{100} = 15:100 = 15\%$$

Changing a Percent to a Ratio

Write 20% as a ratio.

Step 1: Identify the first term.   20 is the first term

Step 2: Identify the second term.   100

Step 3: Write the ratio.   20 out of 100

A ratio can be written in three different ways.

1. With a colon: 20:100

2. As a fraction: $\dfrac{20}{100}$

3. As words: 20 out of 100

Draw a model to represent 20%.

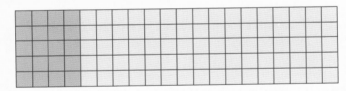

Teach a friend how to change a percent to a ratio or a ratio to a percent. Draw models of your examples.

Remember, % means "per 100." When a percent is written as a ratio, the second term is always 100 (see page 10).

Accountants use decimal equivalents when they are calculating interest.
They have to be able to change percents to decimals and decimals to percents.

Write 35% as a decimal.

Step 1: Place the decimal point to the right of   35.%
the ones digit.

Step 2: Move the decimal point two places to the   0.35
left and drop the percent symbol. Place a zero
before the decimal point to serve as a placeholder.

So, 35% = 0.35

Write 9% as a decimal.

Step 1: Place the decimal point to the right of   9.%
the ones digit.

Step 2: Move the decimal point two places to the   0.09
left. (Add a zero to place the decimal point.)
Drop the percent symbol. Place a zero before
the decimal point to serve as a placeholder.

So, 9% = 0.09

Write 0.5% as a decimal.

Move the decimal point two places to the left. (Add two   0.005
zeros to place the decimal point.) Drop the percent symbol.
Place a zero before the decimal point to serve as a placeholder.

35% means 35 per hundred, or $\frac{35}{100}$, or 35 hundredths.
Remember: Decimals are also ways of writing fractions, so $\frac{35}{100} = 0.35$,
which is 35 hundredths.

Changing a Decimal to a Percent

To change a decimal to a percent, you multiply the decimal by $\frac{100}{100}$. A quick way to do this is to move the decimal point two places to the right and add a percent symbol.

Write 0.069 as a percent.

Move the decimal point two places to the right and add a percent symbol. (This is the same as multiplying by $\frac{100}{100}$)

$0.069 = 6.9\%$

$$0.069 \times \frac{100}{100} = \frac{6.9}{100} = 6.9\%$$

Changing a Mixed Decimal to a Percent

Write 1.75 as a percent.

Move the decimal point two places to the right and add a percent symbol.

$1.75 = 175\%$

Changing a Whole Number to a Percent

Write 4 as a percent.

Step 1: Place a decimal point to the right of the whole number.

4.

Step 2: Move the decimal point two places to the right and add a percent symbol.

$4. = 400\%$

Find out your bank's interest rates on loans and savings accounts. Change these percents to decimals. Who will make more money on $100, you (with a savings account) or the bank (through a loan)?

Multiplying a number by $\frac{100}{100}$ is the same as multiplying it by 1, so the value of the number does not change.

Sometimes stores have clearance sales, where everything is, for example, 20% off. You will need to know what this means to figure out the sale prices of things you want to buy.

Write 20% as a fraction.

Step 1: Write the percent as a fraction. You can do this by placing the whole number in the numerator and placing 100 in the denominator. Drop the percent symbol.

$$20\% = \frac{20}{100}$$

Step 2: Find the greatest common factor (GCF).
factors of 100:   1, 2, 4, 5, 10, **20**, 25, 50, 100
factors of 20:   1, 2, 4, 5, 10, **20**
GCF = 20

Step 3: Reduce the fraction to lowest terms by dividing the numerator and denominator by the GCF.

$$\frac{20 \div 20}{100 \div 20} = \frac{1}{5}$$

20% is the same as $\frac{1}{5}$. The sale price will be $\frac{1}{5}$ less than the regular price.

Changing a Fraction Percent to a Decimal

Write $\frac{1}{2}$% as a decimal.

Step 1: Change the fraction to a decimal by dividing the denominator into the numerator.

$$\begin{array}{r} 0.5 \\ 2\overline{)1.0} \\ -1\,0 \\ \hline 0 \end{array}$$

Remember: 20% means 20 per hundred, or $\frac{20}{100}$. Reduce $\frac{20}{100}$ to lowest terms and you get $\frac{1}{5}$.

Step 2: Move the decimal point two places to the left. Drop the % symbol.

$0.5\% = 0.005$

$\frac{1}{2}\%$ is the same as 0.005.

Changing a Fraction to a Percent

To change a fraction to a percent, multiply the fraction by one hundred percent (or $\frac{100}{100}$) and reduce to lowest terms.

Write $\frac{1}{4}$ as a percent.

Step 1: Multiply the fraction by 100%.

$$\frac{1}{4} \times \frac{100\%}{1} = \frac{100\%}{4}$$

$$\begin{array}{r} 25 \\ 4\overline{)100} \\ -8 \\ \hline 20 \\ -20 \\ \hline 0 \end{array} = 25\%$$

Step 2: Reduce the fraction to lowest terms.

$\frac{1}{4}$ is the same as 25%.

Changing an Improper Fraction to a Percent

Write $\frac{11}{4}$ as a percent.

Step 1: Multiply the improper fraction by 100%.

$$\frac{11}{4} \times \frac{100\%}{1} = \frac{1100\%}{4}$$

Step 2: Reduce the fraction to lowest terms.

$$\begin{array}{r} 275\% \\ 4\overline{)1100} \\ -8 \\ \hline 30 \\ -28 \\ \hline 20 \\ -20 \\ \hline 0 \end{array}$$

$\frac{11}{4}$ is the same as 275%.

An **improper fraction** is a fraction whose numerator is larger than its denominator, such as $\frac{11}{4}$.

Batting averages are expressed as decimals. Suppose your best friend got a hit 32.5% of the time. To find her batting average, change the percent to a decimal.

Changing a Mixed Decimal Percent to a Decimal

To change a mixed decimal percent to a decimal, move the decimal point two places to the left and drop the percent symbol. (See page 38 to find out why this works.)

Write 32.5% as a decimal.

Step 1: Move the decimal point two places to the left and drop the percent symbol. $32.5\% = .325$

Step 2: Place a zero before the decimal point to serve as a placeholder. 0.325

Your best friend's batting average is 0.325.

Changing a Decimal to a Mixed Decimal Percent

Suppose your batting average is 0.345. What percentage of the time do you get a hit when you get up to bat? To change a decimal to a percent, move the decimal two places to the right and add a percent symbol.

Write 0.345 as a percent.

Step 1: Move the decimal 2 places to the right. $0.345 \longrightarrow 34.5$

Step 2: Add the percent symbol. 34.5%

You get a hit 34.5% of the time.

A **mixed numeral** can be written as an improper fraction or a decimal equivalent: $4\frac{1}{2} = \frac{9}{2} = 4.5$.

Changing a Mixed Numeral Percent to a Fraction

To change a mixed numeral percent to a fraction, write the mixed numeral in the numerator and place 100 in the denominator. Drop the percent symbol and reduce the fraction to lowest terms.

Write $83\frac{1}{3}\%$ as a fraction.

Step 1: Place the mixed numeral in the numerator and 100 in the denominator.

$$\frac{83\frac{1}{3}}{100}$$

Step 2: Write a division equation to divide the numerator by the denominator.

$$83\frac{1}{3} \div 100$$

Step 3: Change the mixed numeral to an improper fraction. Write 100 as a fraction by placing it over one.

$$\frac{(83 \times 3) + 1}{3} \div 100 =$$

$$\frac{250}{3} \div \frac{100}{1}$$

Step 4: Find the reciprocal of the divisor.

$$\textbf{divisor} \rightarrow \frac{100}{1}$$

$$\textbf{reciprocal} \rightarrow \frac{1}{100}$$

Step 5: Multiply the improper fraction by the reciprocal of the divisor.

$$\frac{250}{3} \times \frac{1}{100} = \frac{250}{300}$$

Step 6: Reduce the fraction to lowest terms.

$$\frac{250 \div 50}{300 \div 50} = \frac{5}{6}$$

$83\frac{1}{3}\%$ is the same as $\frac{5}{6}$.

To change a mixed numeral, such as $83\frac{1}{3}$, to an improper fraction, multiply the whole number by the denominator, $83 \times 3 = 249$. Then add the numerator — $249 + 1$ — and place it over the denominator: $\frac{250}{3}$.

Finding a percent of a number is used to determine how much you will save or earn on a certain item. Common offers are for 10% off, 6% down payment, and 3% financing.

Finding Percents of Money Amounts

At a school sale, a $30 football is marked 35% off. How much will you save if you buy the football on sale?

What is 35% of $30?

Step 1: Change the percent to a decimal.   35.% = 0.35

Step 2: Multiply. Count the total number of decimal places. Place the decimal point in the product.

0.35	**2 decimal places**
× 30	**0 decimal places**
$10.50	**2 decimal places**

You will save $10.50 if you buy the football on sale.

The sale price of the football will be $30 − $10.50, or $19.50.

Changing Percents to Fractions to Find Amounts

To find a percent of a number, change the percent to a fraction and multiply it by the number.

To review how to change a percent to a decimal, see page 38.

Find $7\frac{2}{3}\%$ of 300.

Step 1: Change the mixed number percent to a fraction.

$$\frac{7\frac{2}{3}}{100}$$

Step 2: Divide the numerator by the denominator.

$$7\frac{2}{3} \div 100$$

dividend ÷ divisor

Step 3: Change the mixed number (dividend) to an improper fraction.

$$\frac{(7 \times 3) + 2}{3} = \frac{23}{3}$$

$$\frac{23}{3} \div 100$$

Step 4: Find the reciprocal of the divisor.

$$\text{divisor} \longrightarrow 100$$
$$\text{reciprocal} \longrightarrow \frac{1}{100}$$

Step 5: Multiply the dividend by the reciprocal of the divisor.

$$\frac{23}{3} \times \frac{1}{100} = \frac{23}{300}$$

$$7\frac{2}{3}\% = \frac{23}{300}$$

Step 6: Multiply $\frac{23}{300}$ by 300. Reduce the numerator and denominator by 300.

$$\frac{23}{\overset{}{\underset{1}{300}}} \times \frac{\overset{1}{300}}{1} = 23$$

$7\frac{2}{3}\%$ of 300 is 23.

The next time you are at your favorite store, write down the percentage off of a sale item. Find out how much you would save if you purchased the item while it was on sale. How much would you spend?

To change a percent to a fraction, drop the percent symbol and place the number over 100.

Your school's hockey team won 36 of the 48 games they played. What percent of its games did the hockey team win?

To find what percent one number is of another,

1. Identify the whole, the part, and the percent.
2. Divide the part by the whole ($\frac{\text{part}}{\text{whole}}$).
3. Multiply the fractional part by 100%.

What percent of the games did the hockey team win?

Step 1: Identify the whole. 48 games

Step 2: Identify the part. 36 games

Step 3: Divide the part by the whole. $\frac{36}{48}$

Step 4: Reduce the fraction to lowest terms. $\frac{36 \div 12}{48 \div 12} = \frac{3}{4}$

Step 5: To change the fraction to a percent, multiply by 100%. Write the multiplication equation. $\frac{3}{4} \times 100\%$

Step 6: Reduce the fractions to lowest terms. Multiply. $\frac{3}{\underset{1}{4}} \times \frac{\overset{25\%}{\cancel{100\%}}}{1} = 75\%$

The hockey team won 75% of its games.

Notice in Step 6, the fractions were reduced before the multiplication. Then you know your answer will be in lowest terms.

Using Ratio and Proportion to Solve Percent Problems

The ratio of the part to the whole is equal to the ratio of the percentage to 100.

$$\frac{part}{whole} = \frac{percentage}{100}$$

What percent of 42 is 28?

Step 1: Identify the part. 28

Step 2: Identify the whole. 42

Step 3: Write the ratio of the part to the whole. $\frac{28}{42}$

Step 4: Let x equal the percentage. $\frac{28}{42} = \frac{x}{100}$

Step 5: Cross multiply. $\frac{28}{42} \diagdown\diagup \frac{x}{100}$

$42x = 2800$

Step 6: Divide both sides by 42 to solve for x. $\frac{42x}{42} = \frac{2800}{42}$

$$\begin{array}{r} 66 \\ 42\overline{)2800} \\ -252 \\ \hline 280 \\ -252 \\ \hline 28 \end{array}$$

Write the remainder as $\frac{28}{42}$, $66\frac{28}{42}$

Step 7: Reduce remainder to lowest terms. $\frac{28 \div 14}{42 \div 14} = \frac{2}{3}$

Step 8: Write the answer as a mixed percent. $66\frac{2}{3}\%$

A **mixed number** consists of a whole number and a fractional part.

Finding the Whole When the Part and Percent Are Given

Your best friend just spent $4.50. This was 15% of all of his money. How much did your best friend have before he spent $4.50?

Step 1: Identify the part. $4.50

Step 2: Identify the percent. Write the percent as a fraction.   15%, or $\frac{15}{100}$

Step 3: Let x = whole. Place the part over the whole and set it equal to the percent. $\frac{\$4.50}{x} = \frac{15}{100}$

Step 4: Cross multiply. $\frac{\$4.50}{x} \diagdown\kern-1.2em\diagup \frac{15}{100}$

$15x = \$450$

$\frac{15x}{15} = \frac{\$450}{15}$

Step 5: Divide by 15 to solve for x.

$$15\overline{)\begin{matrix}\$30. \\ \$450. \\ -45 \\ \hline 0\end{matrix}}$$

Before he spent the $4.50, your best friend had $30.

When finding the whole, let a letter, such as x, stand for the whole.

Sometimes car manufacturers have to recall some of the cars they make because of defective parts.

A car manufacturer recalled 340 cars. This represents 2% of all the cars it manufactured. How many cars did the company manufacture?

Step 1: Identify the part.   340

Step 2: Identify the percent. Write the percent as a fraction.   2%, or $\frac{2}{100}$

Step 3: Let x = whole. Place the part over the whole and set it equal to the percent. $\frac{340}{x} = \frac{2}{100}$

Step 4: Cross multiply.

$$\frac{340}{x} \diagdown\!\!\!\!\diagup \frac{2}{100}$$

$$2x = 340 \times 100$$

$$2x = 34{,}000$$

$$\frac{2x}{2} = \frac{34{,}000}{2}$$

Step 5: Divide by 2 to solve for x.

$$\begin{array}{r} 17{,}000 \\ 2\overline{)34{,}000} \\ \underline{-\ 2} \\ 14 \\ \underline{-\ 14} \\ 0 \end{array}$$

$x = 17{,}000$

The car dealer manufactured 17,000 cars, of which 340 were defective.

Make up a percent problem and give it to a friend or family member to solve. Did they come up with the correct answer?

To check your answer, replace x with the answer. If the fractions are equal, your answer is correct.

Percent increase and decrease are used to show a rise or fall in the value of an item. A percent increase shows a rise, or money earned, over the original amount. A percent decrease shows a drop, or money lost, from the original amount.

Percent Increase

Last year you bought a video game for $20. This year you bought the same video game for your best friend for $25. What is the percent increase in the price?

Step 1: Identify the original price and the new price.

original price = $20
new price = $25

Step 2: Find the difference between the prices.

$25 − $20 = $5

Step 3: Place the difference over the original price.

$\dfrac{\$5}{\$20}$

Step 4: Multiply the fraction by 100%.

$\dfrac{5}{20} \times \dfrac{100\%}{1}$

Step 5: Reduce the fraction to lowest terms.

$\dfrac{5}{\cancel{20}} \times \dfrac{\cancel{100\%}^{5}}{1} = \dfrac{25\%}{1} = 25\%$

The original price of the video game was increased by 25%.

Remember: When finding percent increase or decrease, place the difference over the *original* price, not the *new* price.

Percent Decrease

The student enrollment at your school last year was 500. This year the enrollment is 400 students. What was the percent of decrease in enrollment?

Step 1: Identify the original and the new enrollment.

original = 500
new   = 400

Step 2: Find the difference between the numbers.

$500 - 400 = 100$

Step 3: Place the difference over the original enrollment. Reduce.

$\frac{100}{500} = \frac{1}{5}$

Step 4: Change the fraction to a decimal.

$$\begin{array}{r} 0.20 \\ 5\overline{)1.00} \\ -\underline{1\,0} \\ 0 \end{array}$$

Step 5: Multiply the decimal by 100%.

$0.20 \times 100\% = 20\%$

The percent decrease in enrollment was 20%.

Use a newspaper to compare prices of your favorite CD at different stores. Find the percent of increase or decrease of the CD between stores.

To multiply a decimal by 100%, move the decimal point two places to the right and add the percent symbol.

$$0.20 \times 100\% = 20\%$$

Advertisements in newspapers show discounts and sale prices. The discount is the amount a price has been reduced.

Discount

The terms associated with discount are *regular price* and *discount rate*. The regular price is the cost of the item before it has been reduced. The discount rate is the percent the price has been reduced.

A bike is listed at $150 with a discount of 5%. How much is the discount?

Step 1: Identify the price of the bike. regular price = $150
Identify the discount rate. discount rate = 5%

Step 2: Change the percent to a decimal. 5% = 0.05

Step 3: Multiply the regular price by the discount rate.
Place the decimal point.

150	**0 decimal places**
× 0.05	**2 decimal places**
$7.50	**2 decimal places**

The discount is $7.50.

discount — From *dis* ("to exclude") and *count* ("a number").

Sale Price

A department store advertises 20% off on all sweaters. The regular price of a sweater is $55. What is the sale price?

Step 1: Identify the regular price.
Identify the discount rate.

regular price = $55
discount rate = 20%

Step 2: Change the discount rate to a decimal.

20% = 0.20

Step 3: Find the discount. Multiply the regular price by the discount rate.

$55
× 0.20
discount $11.00

Step 4: Find the difference between the regular price and the discount.

$55 − $11 = $44

The sale price is $44.

Find an ad in a newspaper. What is the regular price of the item? discount rate? discount price? sale price?

To change a percent to a decimal, move the decimal place 2 places to the left and drop the percent symbol.

20% = 0.20

Percents can also be larger than 100%. One hundred percent (100%) is the same as 1 whole; 200% is the same as 2 wholes.

You can draw one square to represent 100% and two squares to represent 200%.

$$■ = 1 \text{ whole}$$
$$■■ = 2 \text{ wholes}$$

Expressing Percents Larger than 100% as Decimals

To express a percent as a decimal, divide the decimal by 100%. You can do this by moving the decimal point two places to the left.

Write 143% as a decimal.

Step 1: Place a decimal point to the right of the ones place.

$$143\% = 143.\%$$

Step 2: Divide by 100%. (Move the decimal point two places to the left and drop the percent symbol.)

$$143.\% = 1.43$$

200% means 2 wholes since 200% is 200 per hundred, or $\frac{200}{100}$. If you reduce $\frac{200}{100}$ you get $\frac{2}{1}$, or 2.

Expressing Decimals as Percents

To express a decimal as a percent, multiply by 100% by moving the decimal point two places to the right.

Write 3.62 as a percent.

Step 1: Multiply the decimal by 100% by moving the decimal point two places to the right and adding a percent symbol.

$$3.62 \times 100\% = 362\%$$

3.62 is the same as 362%.

Expressing Percents Larger than 100% as Fractions

To express a percent as a fraction, divide by 100%. Reduce the fraction to lowest terms.

Write 150% as a fraction.

Step 1: Divide the percent by 100%.

$$\frac{150\%}{100\%}$$

Step 2: Reduce the fraction to lowest terms. Divide by the greatest common factor.

$$\frac{150 \div 50}{100 \div 50} = \frac{3}{2}$$

150% is the same as $\frac{3}{2}$.

Practice changing percents larger than 100% to decimals and fractions with a family member.

Commission and income are two ways people can earn money.

Commission

Commission is the money earned by a salesperson for selling goods. Salespeople are given a certain percentage of money on their total sales.

Suppose you sold magazines. The company pays you 5% of the total sales. Your total sales were $148. How much commission would you earn?

Step 1: Identify the rate of commission.
Identify the total sales.

rate = 5%
total sales = $148

Step 2: Change the commission rate to a decimal. (Move the decimal point two places to the left and drop the percent symbol.)

$5.\% = 0.05$

Step 3: Multiply the total sales by the rate of commission.

$$\begin{array}{r} \$148 \\ \times\ 0.05 \\ \hline \$7.40 \end{array}$$

You would earn a commission of $7.40.

When salespeople receive a certain percent of sales, the amount of money is called a **commission**. The percent is called the **rate of commission**. Here, the rate is 5% and the commission is $7.40.

Income

There are two terms used when we talk about income: gross income and net income. Gross income is the total amount of money earned before deductions are taken. Some deductions taken out from a paycheck are social security, state and federal tax, as well as insurance. Net income is the amount left over after deductions.

Suppose your gross income last year was $500. Find your net income if 6% was taken out for taxes.

Step 1: Identify the gross income. Identify the percent taken out for deductions.

gross income = $500
percent = 6%

Step 2: Change the percent to a decimal. (Move the decimal point two places to the left.)

6% = 0.06

Step 3: Multiply the gross income by the percent to find total deductions.

$500
× 0.06
$30.00

Step 4: Find the difference between the gross income and deductions.

$500 − $30 = $470

Your net income was $470.

Ask a family member for his or her pay stub. Find the gross and net income on the check. How much were their total deductions? What percentage of their gross income was deducted?

When multiplying by a decimal, remember to move the decimal point in the answer to the left the same number of places as there are decimal places in the factors.

27 Simple Interest

Interest is money paid to you by the bank for the use of your money. The money placed in the bank is called the principal. Savings accounts earn a certain rate of interest on the principal.

The percent that the bank will give you is called the rate of interest. The rate of interest is the rate per year. To find simple interest, multiply the principal by the rate of interest by the time.

The equation for simple interest is I = PRT.

I = Simple Interest	P = Principal
R = Rate of Interest	T = Time in years

Time is always measured in years. To change months to years, divide the number of months by 12 months.

For example: 1 month = $\frac{1}{12}$ year   2 months = $\frac{2}{12} = \frac{1}{6}$ year

---

Find the simple interest on $700 for 2 years at 8%.

Step 1: Identify the principal, rate of interest, and time.
P = $700, R = 8%, T = 2 years

Step 2: Change the percent to a decimal.
R = 8.% = 0.08

Step 3: Multiply the principal by the rate by the time.

$$I = P \times R \times T \qquad I = 700 \times 0.08 \times 2$$

$$\begin{array}{r} 700 \\ \times\ 0.08 \\ \hline \$56.00 \end{array} \qquad \begin{array}{r} \$56.00 \\ \times\ 2 \\ \hline \$112.00 \end{array}$$

The simple interest is $112.

Remember: To change a percent to a decimal, move the decimal point 2 places to the left and drop the percent symbol.

There are different terms used for time when finding interest.

Look at the list below:

annually means every 1 year

semiannually means every 6 months $= \frac{6}{12} = 0.5$ year

quarterly means every 3 months $= \frac{3}{12} = 0.25$ year

monthly means every 1 month $= \frac{1}{12}$ year

daily means every 1 day $= \frac{1}{365}$ year

Find the semiannual interest on $800 at 9%.

Step 1: Identify the principal, rate of interest, and time.

$P = \$800, R = 9\%$
$T = 6$ months

Step 2: Change months to years.

$T = \frac{6}{12} = 0.5$

Step 3: Change the percent to a decimal.

$R = 9.\% = 0.09$

Step 4: Multiply the principal by the rate by the time.

$I = PRT$
$I = 800 \times 0.09 \times 0.5$

$$\begin{array}{r} \$800 \\ \times\, 0.09 \\ \hline \$72.00 \\ \times\, 0.5 \\ \hline \$36.000 \end{array}$$

The simple interest is $36.

Find out the interest rate on your savings account. How much will your money earn in a year?

Simple interest is computed only one time on the principal. Compound interest is interest paid on the principal and on the interest. Compound interest is used in savings accounts. You can earn interest on the interest you have already made. Compound interest is the sum of the principal and the interest previously earned.

Find the interest earned if $900 is invested for 1 year at 7% per year compounded twice a year (semiannually).

Step 1: Identify the principal and rate of interest, compounded twice a year.

$P = \$900, R = 7\%$
$T = 6$ months

Step 2: Change months to years.

$T = \dfrac{6}{12} = 0.5$

Step 3: Change the percent to a decimal.

$R = 7\% = 0.07$

Step 4: Multiply the principal by the rate by the time.

$I = PRT$
$I = 900 \times 0.07 \times 0.5$

$$\begin{array}{r} 900 \\ \times\ 0.07 \\ \hline \$63.00 \\ \times\ 0.5 \\ \hline \$31.500 \end{array}$$

Interest for the first 6 months is $31.50

Compound interest is the sum of the principal and the interest previously earned.

Step 5: Add the interest for the first 6 months to the principal.

$900 + 31.50 = \$931.50$
new principal $= \$931.50$

Step 6: Find the interest for the next 6 months using the new principal.

$P = \$931.50$
$R = 7\%$
$T = 0.5$

Step 7: Multiply the new principal by the original rate and time.

$I = \$931.50 \times .07 \times 0.5$

$$
\begin{array}{r}
\$931.50 \\
\times\ .07 \\
\hline
\$65.2050 \\
\times\ 0.5 \\
\hline
\$32.6025
\end{array}
$$

Step 8: Round to the nearest cent.

$\$32.6025$
$\$32.60$

Step 9: Find the sum of the interest.

$$
\begin{array}{lr}
\text{First 6 months} & \$31.50 \\
\text{last 6 months} & +\ \$32.60 \\
\hline
& \$64.10
\end{array}
$$

The compound interest after one year is $64.10

Visit your local bank and find out if they offer simple or compound interest on a savings account.

Compound interest is automatically added to the principal when due.

Further Reading

Books

Ellsbury, Roger. *The Basics of Percents.* New York: Delmar Cengage Learning, 2010.

Wingard-Nelson, Rebecca. *Ratios and Percents (Math Busters).* New Jersey: Enslow Publishers, 2008.

Internet Addresses

Education 4 Kids Inc. Flashcards for Kids. ©1995–2005. <http://www.edu4kids.com/index.php?TB=2&page=12>.

Math2.org. ©1995–2003. <http://www.math2.org/>.

The Math Forum. *Ask Dr. Math.* ©1994–2000. <http://mathforum.org/dr.math/>.

National Council of Teachers of Mathematics. *Figure This! Math Challenges for Families.* ©1999. <http://www.figurethis.org/index40.htm>.

Webmath. n.d. <http://www.webmath.com/k8prop1.html> Webmath. n.d <http://www.webmath.com/k8ratio.html>

ratios
>   and architecture, 30
>   changing to percents, 36
>   and decimals, 20–21
>   equivalent, 12
>   and fractions, 18–19
>   and golden rectangle, 30–31
>   and money, 16
>   order, 7
>   and percents, 10
>   and probability, 32–33
>   and proportion, 24–25, 47
>   reducing, 8, 12–13, 16, 17, 20, 21, 30, 31
>   renaming in higher terms, 13
>   renaming in lowest terms, 12
>   terms, 7, 10, 11, 36, 37
>   and time, 17
>   and units of measure, 16–17
>   whole number, 18–19
>   writing, 6

reduction, 28
renaming ratios, 12–13

S

sale price, 53
scale drawings, 28–29
>   enlargement, 29
>   reduction, 28
simple interest, 58–59

T

terms of ratios, 7, 10, 11, 36, 37
>   unknown, 25, 26–27
time and ratios, 17
true proportion, 24

U

unit pricing, 22–23
units of measure, 16–17

W

whole numbers, 18–19, 39
writing decimals as percents, 39, 42, 55
writing fractions as decimals, 40–41
writing fractions as percents, 41
writing percents as decimals, 38, 54
writing percents as fractions, 40, 43, 44, 55